SIMPLY ME IS THE BEST I CAN BE
NA'AMA GAL

Design
Omer Binder

Production
Niv Books Publishing

Professional guidance by
Literature with Meaning – Mash-Maut

Editing by
Tal Ifergan

Translation by
Grace Michaeli

All Rights Reserved | Copyright © 2021

Printed in Israel 2021

All rights reserved. No part of this book may be reproduced
or used in any manner without written permission of
the copyright owner except for the use of quotations in a book review.

SIMPLY ME
IS THE BEST I CAN BE

Written by: Na'ama Gal

Illustrations by: Noam Marzook

In a faraway land, live families of deer.
Girrafes, bunnies and foxes live without fear.
There are big forests, and fields of green,
clear large lakes where the waters are clean.

Kindy, the little fawn,
played in the meadow for hours,
running and jumping through grass and flowers.

But one thing saddened him,
it was quite unfunny -
he couldn't bounce high
like his good friend Bunny.

He'd been trying for weeks,
but couldn't make it at all,
as hard as he tried,
he would always fall.

Kindy gave up, and went home unhappy and mad,
He was tired, disappointed and feeling rather bad.

He went to his father, low and sad,
"What's the matter, cub?" asked his Dad.

Kindy started crying,
and said through his tears:
"I wanted to bounce high like the bunny,
I tried and tried for weeks, it felt like years!
It hurt all over and it wasn't funny."

Dad listened carefully to his complaining,
then, gently, he started explaining:

"You look sad, and you seem very upset,
you tried so hard to bounce and broke a sweat.
You can't bounce like a bunny, far and high,
but there's no reason that you should try.
Bunny knows how to jump, that much is true,
but fast running and swimming is totally you!"

Kindy felt better after he heard what Dad said,
the sadness was gone, and peace came instead.
Dad suggested with a big smile:
"There's a long-ago story I want to tell,
when I was young and couldn't run well."

"One day, I came home with a big sad frown,
because I ran with my friends, and I fell down.
I told Grandma what happened with a little cry:
'All my friends run so fast, why can't I?'

Your grandma listened, then she thought,
and then said something I never forgot:
'I have a magical phrase for you -
it can fill your heart with joy,
when you're feeling blue!'

Grandma smiled while looking at me:
'Simply me is the best I can be!'

Ever since then, when I'm disappointed or sad,
when I can't succeed like others, and I feel mad,
I just think to myself of that magical phrase,
and become very strong and happy for days."

Kindy smiled.
The feeling was very pleasant,
his Dad had given him an important present.

So as he napped and had an adventurous dream,
he whispered, full of self-esteem:

"Simply me is the best I can be!
Simply me is the best I can be!
Simply me is the best I can be!"

In the morning, when Kindy rose,
he happily ran to where the green grass grows.

On his way, he saw a giraffe by the lakeshore,
she was gloomy and sad, she wept and was sore.

She fell again and again,
while trying to get up and stand.
Why did she fall? She could not understand!
She stayed embarrassed, down on the sand.

Kindy the fawn came close enough to ask:
"Can I help you stand? I'm up for the task!"
She looked up, full of gratitude, and replied:
"Thank you, that would be kind!"

When she stood up and felt safe and sound,
she leaned her head towards Kindy,
her legs strong on the ground.

"I fell down when I tried to drink at the lake,
I couldn't stand up, my legs started to shake.
I wanted to ask for help but was too shy.
Why can they do it, and I can't when I try?"

Kindy remembered how he had felt blue,
thinking of all the things he couldn't do.
And how talking to Dad helped him understand,
how to feel better and reach out to a friend.

"I want to tell you, giraffe, that I also felt bad,
my unpleasant thoughts felt so heavy and sad.
Then my Dad taught me a magical phrase
that helps me feel better on my sad days.
Come, just try and say it with me:

Simply me is the best I can be!"

The giraffe listened to him close and well,
and thought: "Maybe it isn't so bad that I fell.
I can run fast and I have great eyesight..."
Then she immediately felt quite alright.

She stretched her neck, so very long,
and said with a little dance and song:
"A falling giraffe, a sleepy bear or a noisy monkey,
what's important to remember is, you see:

simply me is the best I can be!"

The giraffe was glad, and said in the end:
"Listen, Kindy, you are a true kind of friend!"

The fawn and giraffe already knew,
and soon they could tell all their friends too.
Because it's easy like one two three:

Simply me is the best I can be!

One day they all met by the lake to play,
they were laughing and talking aloud all day.

The Bunny said the woods were far too scary,
and the Elephant was heavy, and it made him quite weary.
The Fox moaned about living in burrows all day,
and the Deer said his big antlers always got in the way.

Kindy and the giraffe remembered suddenly
how they'd felt the same, and told them with glee:
"We have a magical phrase, it even rhymes,
we'll feel better if we say it three times:

Simply me is the best I can be!
Simply me is the best I can be!
Simply me is the best I can be!"

So the Bunny was happy she could skip and jump high,
she could also swim and climb trees as tall as the sky.
And if the woods were scary, so what?
She was brave and shouldn't have to cry.

The Elephant realized he had a great big trunk,
and with it he could bathe, eat and even dunk!
And if he was heavy, then so what?
He wouldn't be happy if he suddenly shrunk!

The Fox was glad his eyes could see through the night,
he could eat almost everything, plus he was bright.
So what if he lived in the burrow all day?
He was great, and his life was just right!

And the Deer was happy to have thin legs, very long,
he could eat plants, and swim — he was so very strong.
So what if his antlers got in the way?
He could skip all day and prance along!

In a faraway land, live families of deer.
Girrafes, bunnies and foxes live without fear.
There are big forests, and fields of green,
clear large lakes where the waters are clean.

And now everyone knows
and says it with glee:

"Simply me is the best I can be!"

Just like Kindy, the little deer,
everyone has learned it loud and clear -
to accept themselves just as they are,
and be kind to others, near or far!

Simply Me is the Best I Can Be

www.ingramcontent.com/pod-product-compliance
Lightning Source LLC
Chambersburg PA
CBHW042126110726
48006CB00003B/786

9 789659 306503